ARE YOU
READY?
Billy Graham

DO YOU REALLY BELIEVE THAT JESUS CHRIST IS GOING TO COME BACK TO THIS EARTH AGAIN?

I do. And I don't see any other hope for the world because we're heading toward a catastrophe.

The Bible says, "Scoffers will come in the last days. . . . They will say, 'Where is the promise of his coming?' For they deliberately overlook this fact, that the heavens existed long ago, and the earth was formed out of water and through water by the word of God, and that by means of these the world that then existed was deluged with water and perished. But by the same word the heavens and earth that now exist are stored up for fire, being kept until the day of judgment and destruction of the ungodly" (2 Peter 3:3–7).

Today the only bright spot on the horizon of this world's future is the promise of the return of Jesus Christ. We can't go on like this much longer, either morally or scientifically. The technology that was supposed to save us is ready to destroy us. Yet we're not to wait in terror, because as Christians, we have the hope of the return of Christ. When is he going to return? Jesus said, "Concerning that day and hour no one knows, not even the angels of heaven, nor the Son, but the Father only" (Matthew 24:36).

"NOAH BELIEVED IN GOD, AND TRUE FAITH DETERMINED HOW HE LIVED. TRUE FAITH SHOULD DETERMINE HOW WE LIVE, TOO."

But are you ready when the end of life in this world comes for you personally? The Bible says, "It is appointed for man to die once, and after that comes judgment" (Hebrews 9:27). It is coming the moment you die, and that could be at any time for any of us. You may be expecting to live for many more years, but you can't know for sure. We never know. One of the biblical prophets wrote, "Prepare to meet your God" (Amos 4:12). What have you done spiritually in your life to prepare for that moment when your heart stops beating? The Bible also says about Jesus: "There is salvation [from God's judgment for sin] in no one else, for there is no other name under heaven given among men by which we must be saved" (Acts 4:12). You need to make a commitment to Christ today.

First, repent of your sins, including all of those things we say and do that offend other people, and God himself! "All have sinned and fall short of the glory of God" (Romans 3:23). Without God's Spirit coming to live within us we don't have the strength to change and live a life that pleases God. That's why we need to be saved! Repentance means that you say to God, "I have sinned. I am sorry for my sins. I want to change my way of living by your empowerment."

The Word of God, the Bible, speaks of the certainties of the end of the world. Jesus said, “As were the days of Noah, so will be the coming of the Son of Man” (Matthew 24:37). What were the days of Noah like? And is there a parallel for today? The people of Noah’s day were very wicked: “Every intention of the thoughts” of their hearts was “only evil continually” (Genesis 6:5). Marriage was abused, people were corrupt, violence prevailed (Genesis 6:1–13). There was a lot of “religion,” but it was decadent. People were preoccupied with things and didn’t have time for God.

So God warned them, “Unless you repent and change your ways, you’re going to face judgment.” In the middle of all that corruption, Noah dared to live for God. Noah believed in God, and true faith determined how he lived. By that faith Noah built a ship in the middle of the desert, and he and his family were saved when the waters of destruction came (Genesis 6:1–13, Hebrews 11:7). True faith should determine how we live, too.

Second, you come to God by faith. That means that you put your whole trust in him and say, "Lord, I believe Christ's death for me provides everything I need to be forgiven for my sins and become accepted by you. I trust in Jesus alone for my salvation. Please save me now and help me live for you."

You may be a good person. You may do all the good that you can think of, but all of that isn't enough. You must come in childlike faith to Jesus who died on the cross for you, who rose again, who is waiting for you to make that commitment.

ARE YOU READY TO MEET GOD?

CROSSWAY

GOOD NEWS *Tracts*

www.goodnewstracts.org

ISBN 978-1-68216-321-4

50299

9 781682 163214